The Ice Cream Sundae Book

The Ice Cream Sundae Book

A Step-by-Step Guide to Making America's Favorite Dessert

MICHAEL TURBACK

Photography by Bonnie Matthews

Skyhorse Publishing

Library of Congress Cataloging-in-Publication Data is available on file.

Cover design by Daniel Brount
Cover photo by Bonnie Matthews

Print ISBN: 978-1-5107-4923-8
Ebook ISBN: 978-1-5107-4924-5

Printed in China

*To Chester C. Platt (1869–1934) who, on April 3, 1892,
invented the ice cream sundae in Ithaca, New York.*

Contents

Introduction

More than any other native dish, the ice cream sundae is a reminder of the American genius for invention. It's like no other dessert in the world—a grand idea that could only be conceived in a place as grand as America. For well over a century, the sundae has been an enduring symbol of our abundance and appetite, our ingenuity, and our never-lost youth.

Sundaes are us, and they have been pleasuring our collective senses ever since 1892, when an enterprising soda fountain proprietor in Ithaca, New York, accessorized a scoop of ice cream with sweet syrup and a candied cherry, then named it after the day it was invented.

In their assembly, sundaes provide an unrestrained opportunity to express our essential character. They acquire personality not only through their combination of ingredients, but through the history they witness. During the twists and turns our country has taken over the past hundred plus years, ice cream sundaes have been standing by to lift our spirits. After the 1929 stock market crash, one of the few luxuries average folks could afford was the democratically priced sundae. During World War II, patriotic "Victory Sundaes" included a Defense Saving Stamp with every purchase, while the Navy commissioned floating ice cream parlors (refrigerated barges with ice cream plants) to boost troop morale. In wartime and in hard times, home refrigerators were stocked with ice creams that, with a dash of imagination, provided the basis for an irresistible sundae.

Following the classic model, sundaes are served with scoops of ice cream as the foundation for interplays of sauces or syrups, perhaps the crunch of nuts, and often a cloud of whipped cream and signature cherry. It was Somerset Maugham who wrote "Tradition is a guide and not a jailer," and that explains our unremitting playfulness with sundae formulas over the years.

In the 1942 *Soda Fountain Handbook*, a professional program for the soda fountain trade, editor Mal Parks explains "If you have an inherent talent for improvisation, your greatest outlet is in the field dealing with sundaes. With just a few simple syrups and the variety of toppings you have on your soda fountain, you can turn out an exhaustive array of possible combinations."

The following pages provide a scholarly glimpse into sundae culture—from humble, forgotten relics to dishes that have become popular standards. Offered here is a collection of authentic formulas for the assembly of plain and fancy sundaes and the preparation of homemade ice creams and toppings. This tour de force represents a cross section of the discipline, drawing from a range of vintage and contemporary sources to create a definitive catalog of the greatest American ice cream sundaes.

But this is more than just a collection of dessert recipes. Think of it as a culinary adventure story—with a cherry on top. On every page there is a morsel of sociology and a smidgen of history, all in aid of explaining the uniquely Americanness of the sundae.

About the Author

Michael Turback lives in Ithaca, New York, the birthplace of the ice cream sundae. His very first book, *A Month of Sundaes*, became a bestseller. A follow-up work, *The Banana Split Book*, celebrated the 100th anniversary of the dish in Latrobe, Pennsylvania. He has appeared on national TV, making sundaes with Jane Clayson on *CBS This Morning*, with Charles Grodin on *60 Minutes II*, and with Steve Hartman on "Assignment America" during the *CBS Evening News*. Michael is a nationally known culinary and mixological historian. He is obsessed with the craft of the ice cream sundae.

About the Photographer

Bonnie Matthews is a food photographer, illustrator, and author of *The Freekeh Cookbook*, *Hot & Hip Grilling Secrets*, *Hot & Hip Healthy Gluten-Free Cooking*, *The Eat Your Way Healthy at Trader Joe's Cookbook*, and *The Healthy 5-Ingredient Air Fryer Cookbook*. She has photographed numerous cookbooks in *The New York Times* bestselling Fix-It and Forget-It series including *Fix-It and Forget-It Holiday Favorites* and *Fix-It and Forget-It Healthy Slow Cooker Cookbook*, among others.

When Bonnie is not creating recipes or photographing food, she's drawing and painting for children's books and magazines. She's illustrated twenty-five books for children, including the award-winning What to Do series. In her spare time, she escapes to tiny islands and snorkels to get inspiration for the characters she draws. She lives in Costa Mesa, California.

Sundae Bases

Brownies

¼ cups semisweet chocolate
1 pound (4 sticks) butter
3 cups granulated sugar
1 cup cake flour
1 tablespoon baking powder
4 whole eggs
2 cups crushed walnuts

Makes 24 brownies

DIRECTIONS

Preheat the oven to 300°F. Melt the chocolate with the butter in a double boiler. Mix the sugar, flour, and baking powder together in a bowl. Mix the chocolate with the flour mixture, about 4 to 5 minutes. Add the eggs and mix.

Pour the mixture into a 9 x 13-inch baking pan. Sprinkle the walnuts on top, pressing the walnuts down slightly into the mixture with your hand. Bake for 30 to 40 minutes. After removing from the oven, allow to cool about 30 minutes.

Pound Cake

Makes 16 slices

DIRECTIONS

Sift the flour, baking soda, and baking powder into a mixing bowl. Stir in salt and the sugar, then add the butter. Add the eggs and begin mixing on slow. Gradually add the buttermilk, then the vanilla extract. Turn the mixer up to medium for a few minutes, then finally to high.

Preheat oven to 325°F. Oil a tube cake pan with butter. Lightly flour the oiled pan, then shake the excess flour from the pan. Pour mix into the pan and bake for about 1 hour and 20 minutes. Allow the cake to cool 15 or 20 minutes in the pan, then gently remove it to a cake plate.

3 cups cake flour + extra for coating the pan
½ teaspoon baking soda
1 teaspoon baking powder
½ teaspoon salt
1 pound sugar
1 pound butter, softened to room temperature + extra for coating the pan
6 large eggs
½ cup buttermilk
2 teaspoons of pure vanilla extract

Homemade Ice Creams

Old-Fashioned Vanilla

6

Philadelphia Vanilla

7

Chocolate

8

Strawberry

9

Coffee

10

**Please note that all homemade ice creams
require an ice cream maker**

Old-Fashioned Vanilla

2 eggs

1 (14 ounce) can sweetened condensed milk

¼ cup sugar

¼ cup brown sugar

2 cups heavy cream

2 cups half-and-half

Salt

2½ tablespoons pure vanilla extract

Makes 1½ quarts

DIRECTIONS

In a large mixing bowl, whisk eggs. Add condensed milk and whisk together until thoroughly mixed. Add sugar and brown sugar and again mix thoroughly. Then, add heavy cream, half-and-half, a pinch of salt, and vanilla extract. Let the mix chill in the refrigerator for about 4 hours to allow the mixture to age, then freeze, following the directions of your ice cream maker.

Philadelphia Vanilla

Makes 1½ quarts

2 cups heavy cream
1 cup milk
¾ cup sugar
1 teaspoon vanilla extract

DIRECTIONS

In a large mixing bowl combine all ingredients until well blended. Freeze, following the instructions of your ice cream maker. To make a fruity ice cream, add ½ cup of coarsely chopped fruit during the last few minutes of freezing.

Chocolate

2 cups heavy cream
1 cup milk
½ cup chocolate syrup

Makes 1½ quarts

DIRECTIONS

In a large mixing bowl combine the ingredients in the order listed until well blended. Freeze, following the instructions of your ice cream machine. This recipe can be made into double-chocolate ice cream by stirring in ¾ cup of semisweet chocolate mini-chips ten or fifteen minutes before ice cream freezing time is over.

Strawberry

Makes 1½ quarts

DIRECTIONS

Clean and destem the strawberries and cut them into bite-sized pieces. Add sugar and the juice of the half lemon. Let strawberries marinate in the refrigerator overnight or at least 4 hours. When the Old-Fashioned Vanilla ice cream mix has been sufficiently chilled and is ready for use, strain the strawberries, reserving the juice. Place the strawberries in the freezer compartment of your refrigerator. Combine the strawberry syrup and vanilla cream. Freeze the ice cream mix, following the rules of your ice cream maker. When the ice cream is almost frozen, add the strawberries and finish freezing.

2 pints fresh, ripe strawberries
½ cup sugar
½ lemon
1½ quarts Old-Fashioned
  Vanilla ice cream (page 6)
  (refrigerated for 4 hours)

Coffee

2½ cups whole milk

1½ cups granulated sugar

⅛ teaspoon salt

2 tablespoons instant coffee granules

6 egg yolks

2¼ cups heavy cream

1½ teaspoons vanilla extract

Makes 1½ quarts

DIRECTIONS

In a medium saucepan, combine the milk, sugar, salt, and coffee granules. Cook over medium heat, stirring occasionally until steaming. Reduce the heat to low. Lightly beat the egg yolks in a small bowl. Slowly pour half the hot milk into the eggs while whisking continuously. Return the mixture to the pot and cook over medium heat, stirring occasionally, until thickened, about 5 minutes. Strain the custard through a fine-mesh sieve set over a medium bowl. Refrigerate until cold. When ready to make the ice cream, whisk the cream and vanilla into the custard until smooth. Freeze according to instructions of your ice cream maker.

Toppings

Hot Fudge

12

Hot Butterscotch

13

Strawberry Sauce

14

Marshmallow Sauce

15

Melba Sauce

16

Chocolate Syrup

17

Caramel Syrup

18

Coffee Syrup

19

Whipped Cream

20

Wet Walnuts

21

Roasted Almonds

22

Hot Fudge

1 tablespoon unsweetened
   cocoa powder
1 cup sugar
¾ cup heavy cream, divided
¼ cup light corn syrup
2 tablespoons unsalted butter
2 ounces unsweetened
   chocolate, chopped
1 teaspoon vanilla extract
Salt
Malt vinegar

Makes 2 cups

DIRECTIONS

In a heavy, medium saucepan over medium heat, whisk together the cocoa, sugar, and ¼ cup of the heavy cream until smooth, about 2 minutes. Stir in the corn syrup, butter, unsweetened chocolate bits, and remaining ½ cup heavy cream, and bring to a boil. Remove from the heat and stir in the vanilla, a pinch of salt, and a few drops of malt vinegar.

Sauce may be refrigerated in an airtight container for up to 3 weeks. To reheat, set over a double boiler, whisking vigorously. If reheating over direct heat, use very low flame, and be careful not to let the sauce bubble or burn.

Hot Butterscotch

Makes 2 cups

DIRECTIONS

In a heavy, medium saucepan, combine the brown sugar, corn syrup, butter, and salt. Bring to a boil, stirring constantly over medium heat, and cook for 1 minute. Turn off the heat and stir in the cream, then stir in the vanilla. Allow to cool slightly (mixture will be very hot). Serve warm.

1 cup packed light brown sugar
½ cup light corn syrup
6 tablespoons (¾ stick) unsalted butter
⅛ tablespoon salt
½ cup heavy cream
½ teaspoon vanilla extract

Strawberry Sauce

2 quarts fresh, sweet strawberries

1 cup sugar (or a little more if berries are tart)

Makes 2 cups

DIRECTIONS

Wash, destem, and crush berries using a potato masher or fork, and crust lightly with sugar. Let set for at least 1 hour to allow berries to macerate and release their juice. Transfer sweetened berries and juice to a large, heavy saucepan and carefully bring to a simmer. Cook, stirring often, for about 12 to 15 minutes or until slightly thickened.

Marshmallow Sauce

Makes 3 cups

2 large egg whites
1 cup sugar
½ cup water
16 regular marshmallows
¼ teaspoon vanilla extract

DIRECTIONS

Using an electric mixer, beat egg whites in a mixing bowl on medium speed until soft peaks form, about 2 to 3 minutes. Set aside.

Combine sugar and water in a medium-size saucepan and place over medium heat. Stir until sugar dissolves. Once sugar is dissolved, stop stirring and allow sugar/water mixture to come to a boil. Boil for 3 minutes without stirring.

Reduce heat to low, add marshmallows, and stir until they are completely melted and mixture is smooth, about 4 minutes.

Remove from heat and, using the electric mixer on low speed, beat hot marshmallow mixture into the egg whites. Continue beating for 2 minutes. Beat in vanilla. Serve warm or cold. Sauce may be refrigerated in an airtight container for up to 3 weeks. To reheat, microwave on low power for 30 seconds, or until warm.

Melba Sauce

1 cup fresh raspberries
¼ cup sugar

Makes 1 cup

DIRECTIONS

Force raspberries through a sieve fine enough to hold back the seeds. Place into a saucepan, add sugar, and cook over moderate heat for 10 minutes, or long enough to make a heavy sauce. Serve cold.

Chocolate Syrup

Makes 1 cup

DIRECTIONS

Melt chocolate in top of a double boiler. Gradually stir in evaporated milk, and continue stirring until sauce is fully blended and smooth. Remove from heat and stir in water until smooth. Syrup may be refrigerated in an airtight container for up to 3 weeks. To reheat, set over a double boiler and stir until smooth. If reheating over direct heat, use very low flame, and be careful not to let the sauce bubble or burn.

6 ounces semisweet chocolate
½ cup evaporated milk
¼ cup water

Caramel Syrup

1 cup granulated sugar
⅓ cup water
1 cup heavy cream

Makes 1 cup

DIRECTIONS

Combine sugar and water in a heavy, medium-size saucepan. Stir constantly over medium heat until sugar is dissolved and the mixture comes to a boil. Stop stirring and boil until the mixture turns a deep caramel color (6 to 12 minutes). Watch carefully to make sure mixture doesn't get too dark.

Remove from heat and add cream (caution: mixture will bubble up fiercely). Return pan to high heat and boil, stirring occasionally, for 2 minutes. Remove from heat and pour into a glass measuring cup or other heatproof container. Allow to cool to desired temperature. Syrup can be refrigerated in an airtight container for up to 3 weeks. To reheat, microwave on low power at 15-second intervals, or until warm.

Coffee Syrup

Makes 1 cup

1 cup sugar
1 cup extra-strength brewed
coffee

DIRECTIONS

Combine sugar and coffee in a medium saucepan. Bring to a boil, stirring constantly to dissolve sugar. Lower heat and simmer for 3 minutes, stirring often.

Whipped Cream

1 cup heavy cream
¼ cup sweetened condensed
  milk

Makes 2 cups

DIRECTIONS

Combine heavy whipping cream and condensed milk (both well-chilled) in a metal mixing bowl. Whip with a handheld electric mixer at medium-high speed. To incorporate the most air, move the beaters up, down, and around the sides of the bowl during whipping. When the cream has doubled in volume and forms stiff peaks, you are ready to add a dramatic swirl to a sundae.

The richer the cream, the more air it will trap and hold. Most recipes call for confectioner's sugar, but sweetened condensed milk makes a more stable whipped cream.

Wet Walnuts

Makes 2 cups

¾ cup corn syrup

½ cup pure maple syrup

½ cup granulated sugar

¼ cup water

1¼ cups coarsely chopped
  walnuts

DIRECTIONS

In a saucepan, combine the corn syrup, maple syrup, sugar, and water and place it over medium heat. Bring to a boil, stirring occasionally. Stir in the nuts, reduce the heat, and simmer uncovered for about 25 minutes or until thick.

Roasted Almonds

1 cup fresh almonds
1 tablespoon extra-virgin
   olive oil
½ teaspoon sea salt

Place almonds in a single layer on flat pan or cookie sheet. Add the oil and toss to coat evenly. Roast in a preheated 325°F oven for 20 to 30 minutes, stirring occasionally. Remove from oven and sprinkle with salt.

Sundaes

Hot Fudge Sundae

The world's first hot fudge sundaes were served at Clarence Clifton Brown's Hollywood, California, ice cream parlor in 1906. Your server scooped vanilla ice cream into a silver goblet, then added a dollop of whipped cream and a sprinkling of chopped roasted almonds. Small brown ceramic pitchers filled with hot fudge were kept in a hot-water bath until an order was placed, then served on the side. You could pour it over the top of the ice cream in one fell swoop, or parcel it out over the course of eating your sundae.

DIRECTIONS

Into a tulip sundae glass, put 1 ounce of hot fudge. Add the vanilla ice cream. Top with whipped cream and sprinkle with almonds. Fill a small pitcher with remaining hot fudge and serve on the side.

6 ounces hot fudge sauce (page 12), divided
2 scoops vanilla ice cream (page 6)
Whipped cream (page 20)
Roasted almonds (page 22), chopped

Situated half a block from Mann's Chinese Theater, C.C. Brown's became a popular gathering place for celebrities like Mary Pickford, Joan Crawford, and Bob Hope as well as regular folks looking for a treat after a night out at the movies.

From St. Louis–based *Meyer Brothers Druggist* (1918): "The boy of today knows that the girl of today wants the dishes of today (ice cream) whether the weather is hot or cold, says the Soda Dispenser. In the winter she likes it best with a nice warm dressing. Install a fudge set if you have not already done so."

Dusty Road Sundae

4 ounces chocolate syrup
(page 17), divided
2 scoops coffee ice cream
(page 10)
1 tablespoon + ½ teaspoon
malted milk powder
Whipped cream (page 20)

Originally manufactured in the 1870s by William and James Horlick as an infant food, malted milk became better known as the toasty flavoring in double-rich chocolate malted milkshakes offered at Walgreens drugstore lunch counters, beginning with the invention of the electric blender in 1922. As malts became universally popular soda fountain drinks, it wasn't long before malted milk powder was employed as a "dusty" topping for the chocolate sundae.

DIRECTIONS

Into a tulip sundae glass put 1 ounce of the chocolate syrup. Add the coffee ice cream. Cover with remaining chocolate syrup. Top with 1 tablespoon of malted milk powder, then whipped cream. Dust with ½ teaspoon of malted milk powder.

According to the 1938 *Borden's Formulary for Soda Fountain Operators*, a similar fountain formula was called the Jersey Special.

From *The International Confectioner* (1919): "A menu should be more than a list, and an unintelligible one at that. Let your menu talk your beverages and sundaes. Like the sign when it gives a name, it should give a tempting description of the item."

Dusty Miller Sundae

Early drugstore soda fountains promoted the combination of ice cream and malted milk as a complete meal, citing its use as a provision for the era, and South Pole expeditions by Robert Peary, Roald Amundsen, and Robert Falcon Scott. Before long, Horlick's, the original manufacturer of malted milk, was being widely imitated by rivals including Carnation and Borden's. In soda fountain slang, malted milk was often called "hops," and the Dusty Road Sundae spawned a hops-topped cousin called Dusty Miller.

DIRECTIONS

Into a tulip sundae glass put 1 ounce of the chocolate syrup. Add the vanilla ice cream. Cover with remaining chocolate syrup, then the marshmallow sauce. Top with 1 tablespoon of malted milk powder, then whipped cream. Dust with ½ teaspoon of malted milk powder.

> "Malt shops" owe their very name to the Horlick brothers, two British men who started out to make a malted milk drink for infants.

> In 1922, Polish-born Stephen Poplawski had the brilliant idea of putting a rotating blade at the bottom of a container. He invented the electric blender for the specific use of allowing milkshakes and malts to be made easily at home.

3 ounces chocolate syrup (page 17), divided

2 scoops vanilla ice cream (page 6)

2 ounces marshmallow sauce (page 15)

1 tablespoon + ½ teaspoon malted milk powder, divided

Whipped cream (page 20)

Tin Roof Sundae

4 ounces chocolate syrup
   (page 17), divided
2 scoops vanilla ice cream
⅓ cup salted peanuts, fresh-
   roasted

In 1908 John E. Wirt, a young pharmacist working at the A.R. Keep drugstore in Meadville, Pennsylvania, decided that chocolate syrup and salted peanuts over a scoop of ice cream in a glass would attract more business to the store's soda fountain. He already knew that when salt and sweet are simultaneously applied to the tongue, each sensation is enhanced by the other. Wirt christened his creation the "tin roof," although over the years some have insisted on renaming the sundae a "Mexican."

DIRECTIONS

Into a tulip sundae glass put 1 ounce of the chocolate syrup. Add the vanilla ice cream. Cover with remaining chocolate syrup. Top with a layer of peanuts.

Salted Spanish peanuts are recommended for this dish, though chocolate syrup also teams beautifully with any other nut combination.

Howard Lake Drug, one of the oldest drugstores in Minnesota, still has the original tin ceiling and counter fixtures. The seven-stool soda fountain features a Midwest version of the Tin Roof Sundae called the "Mudball."

Banana Skyscraper

While the banana split has maintained no fixed formula over the decades, it has always leaned toward the offbeat. From its 1904 beginnings, the idea of slicing a tropical banana from stem to stern as a base for ice creams and syrups has captured the imaginations of soda fountaineers. In 1936, Penn Pharmacy, near the University of Pennsylvania campus, first served a twice-sliced banana, skillfully placed upright in a sundae goblet, adding a stunning new dimension to the traditional split.

DIRECTIONS

Into a tall tulip sundae glass put the chocolate syrup. Add the vanilla ice cream. Split the banana lengthwise, then cut the split halves again widthwise. Place the banana quarters, cut-side out, into the glass and add the chocolate ice cream, keeping the banana pieces in place. Cover with the crushed strawberries. Top with whipped cream, garnish with cherry.

At Edgar's Fountain (Pioneer Drug) in Elk Point, South Dakota, a vertical banana split is called The Rocket.

4 ounces chocolate syrup (page 17), divided

1 scoop vanilla ice cream

1 banana, peeled

1 scoop chocolate ice cream (page 8)

4 ounces crushed strawberries

Whipped cream (page 20)

1 maraschino cherry

1 scoop vanilla ice cream

1 scoop chocolate ice cream
   (page 8)

1 slice pound cake (page 3)

4 ounces hot fudge (page 12)

4 ounces marshmallow sauce
   (page 15)

Whipped cream (page 20)

Mixed nuts, chopped

2 maraschino cherries

It was Portland, Oregon, in 1963, where Bob Farrell opened the first of what would become a chain of ice cream "parlours," re-creating a segment of one of the most colorful and memorable eras in American history—the Gay Nineties (1890s, that is). Staff members dressed in period pinstriped vests and cane hats, while player pianos belted out ragtime melodies. If it was your birthday, sirens wailed as a sundae was delivered to your table, free of charge! "Two on a Blanket" was a pound cake–based Farrell's original, featuring the yin and yang of vanilla and chocolate.

DIRECTIONS

Place 1 large scoop each of vanilla and chocolate ice cream side by side on a slice of toasted pound cake. Cover the vanilla ice cream with hot fudge and chocolate with marshmallow sauce. Top with whipped cream, sprinkle with the chopped mixed nuts, and garnish with cherries.

From *Emily Post's Advice for Every Dining Occasion*: "Ice cream is generally eaten with a spoon, but when accompanied by cake, either the spoon alone or both the spoon and fork may be used."

Butterscotch Sundae

Bailey's was a Boston ice cream shop, opened in 1873 by candymakers John B. Bailey and D. H. Page, originally selling candy bars, chocolates, and other confections. Bailey's of Boston became an ice cream parlor, eventually with as many as a dozen locations in and around the city. It was the home of legendary butterscotch sundaes, served in silver-plated pedestal dishes set on small round silver plates to catch the rich sauce that always dripped down from the dish. The secret was a base of coffee ice cream, cutting the sweetness of the sauce, and a final crowning of whipped cream and salted walnuts.

4 ounces hot butterscotch (page 13), divided
2 scoops coffee ice cream (page 10)
Whipped cream (page 20)
Salted walnuts, toasted

DIRECTIONS

Into a tulip sundae glass put 1 ounce of butterscotch. Add coffee ice cream. Cover with remaining butterscotch. Top with whipped cream and sprinkle with the walnuts.

Andy Warhol on the Beverly Hills shopping district: "Rodeo Drive is a giant Butterscotch Sundae."

The venerable Bailey's of Boston was once an important stop on any shopping trip to Jordan Marsh, Gilchrist's, R. H. Stearns, or other long-forgotten downtown department stores.

Turtle Sundae

3 ounces chocolate syrup
(page 17), divided

3 ounces caramel syrup (page
18), divided

2 scoops chocolate ice cream
(page 8)

Whipped cream (page 20)

Salted pecans, toasted

The turtle candy was first offered to the public in the early 1920s by Chicago confectioner Rowntree DeMet. An employee at his chocolate factory remarked that a new treat, chocolate-coated caramel with pecans protruding from its side, looked a lot like a turtle. The name stuck, and as the candy became a staple in the Midwest, it wasn't long before the marvelous combination of sweet, salty, and creamy chocolate was embraced at ice cream parlors and a new sundae was born.

DIRECTIONS

Into a tulip sundae glass, put 1 ounce chocolate and 1 ounce caramel syrups. Add the chocolate ice cream. Cover with remaining chocolate and caramel syrups. Top with whipped cream and sprinkle with the pecans.

Toasting the nuts creates a deeper and richer flavor, and adding a dash of salt is always a good counterpoint to this sweet dish.

The Turtle Sundae is a miracle of synergy, in the hands of gifted fountaineers, as cohabiting sauces assume the elegance of perfect poetry.

Brown Derby

1 doughnut
1 scoop chocolate ice cream
  (page 8)
4 ounces chocolate syrup
  (page 17)
Whipped cream (page 20)
1 maraschino cherry

Who put the hole in the doughnut? It was a sea captain from Rockport, Maine, who poked out the centers of his wife's fried cakes so that he could slip them over the spokes of his ship's wheel, allowing him to nibble while keeping an even keel. The hole provides a perfect vehicle for "dunking," and in soda fountain slang, an order for doughnuts and coffee came out "sinkers and suds." When a chocolate doughnut becomes a base for chocolate ice cream with chocolate syrup, it's called a Brown Derby. (At the Dairy Dome in Stoneham, Massachusetts, freshly fried dough becomes the base for vanilla ice cream with caramel in a Fried Dough Sundae).

DIRECTIONS

Place doughnut at the center of a flat dish. Add chocolate ice cream on top of the doughnut. Cover with chocolate syrup. Top with whipped cream and garnish with cherry.

Chocolate topping for sundaes and specials should be twice as heavy as chocolate syrup used in sodas.

Opened in 1929, the Brown Derby was a landmark restaurant in Los Angeles, California, frequented by celebrities during the Golden Age of Hollywood. The shape of the building was inspired by Al Smith's derby hat.

Scotch & Fudge

2 scoops vanilla ice cream
(page 6)
3 ounces hot fudge (page 12)
3 ounces hot butterscotch
(page 13)
Whipped cream (page 20)
2 maraschino cherries

For many years, the Howard Johnson name was part of American popular culture. It all started in 1925 at a small corner drugstore across from the Wollaston railroad station in Quincy, Massachusetts. Young Mr. Johnson discovered that the soda fountain was the most profitable part of his venture, a consequence of the popularity of his butterfat-rich ice cream. He opened concession stands along area beaches, then opened the first of what would eventually become a chain of more than 1,000 restaurants and 500 motor lodges in 42 states and in Canada. One of Howard Johnson's early sundaes featured twin scoops of ice cream, originally with vanilla ice cream, later with peppermint stick ice cream.

DIRECTIONS

Add scoops of vanilla ice cream side by side in an oval dish. Cover one scoop with hot fudge, cover the other with butterscotch. Top with whipped cream and garnish with cherries.

According to *White's Vest Pocket Sundae Formulary*, a similar fountain formula was called the Fifty-Fifty Sundae.

Instructions on sundaes from the *Howard Johnson's Fountain Service Manual*: "Place a #16 conical scoop of ice cream in a sundae dish. (This should be well molded into the dish to keep it upright at all times) and cover with proper amount of syrup, sauce, or fruit."

Bachelor's Kiss

Back in 1908, Angelo Lagomarcino, an immigrant from Northern Italy, founded an eponymous confectionary in Moline, Illinois, operating the business with his wife Luigia and their three children Charlie, Mary, and Tom. In 1912, Angelo paid a traveling salesman twenty-five dollars for a hot fudge recipe that became the centerpiece of his sundae offerings. Things haven't changed much at Lagomarcino's. You can still slide into one of the original handcrafted mahogany booths for the Batchelor's Kiss, a double-dip sundae that encourages sharing (made with the celebrated hot fudge, of course).

1 scoop vanilla ice cream (page 6)
1 scoop chocolate ice cream (page 8)
3 ounces hot fudge (page 12)
3 ounces marshmallow sauce (page 15)
Whipped cream (page 20)
2 maraschino cherries

DIRECTIONS

Add scoops of vanilla and chocolate ice creams side by side in an oval dish. Cover the vanilla ice cream with hot fudge, cover the chocolate with marshmallow sauce. Top with whipped cream and garnish with cherries.

From *The Pacific Drug Review* (1920): Serve a glass of water with every sundae whether requested or not.

H. L. Mencken, the cranky Baltimore newspaperman, hated the ice cream sundae. He called the "misspelled" dessert a "soda fountain mess," and concluded that it was precisely the strange spelling that was responsible for its popularity.

6 ounces hot fudge (page 12),
   divided
2 scoops coffee ice cream
   (page 10)
Whipped cream (page 20)
Roasted almonds (page 22),
   chopped
White chocolate, shaved

Walter C. Mundt immigrated to America from Germany in 1866, securing a position with confectioners A&J Doescher in Cincinnati, Ohio. In 1886 he made the wedding cake for twenty-eight-year-old William Howard Taft (who would be elected president of the United States twenty-two years later), and he supervised the making of ice cream and confections at the 1888 Ohio Centennial Exposition. In 1893 Walter moved his family to Madison, Wisconsin, where he founded Mundt's Candies. True to tradition, the Army-Navy Sundae at Mundt's is served with a "pitcherette" of hot fudge and a French wafer on the side.

DIRECTIONS

Into a tulip sundae glass put 1 ounce hot fudge. Add the coffee ice cream. Top with whipped cream and sprinkle with almonds and white chocolate. Fill a small pitcher with remaining hot fudge and serve on the side.

The "pitcherette" on the side allows you to pour the fudge over the top of the ice cream in one fell swoop or parcel it out over the course of eating your sundae.

From *The Bulletin of Pharmacy* (1919): "Hot fudge should not be poured over the ice cream until just before placing it in front of the customer. Some stores, indeed, serve the dressing in a separate pitcher, a practice which allows the customer to mix the sundae as he wishes."

Don't Care Sundae

Schwab's Drugstore on Sunset Boulevard in Hollywood, California, was once the meeting place of movie actors and dealmakers. During its lifespan from the 1930s through the 1950s, insiders referred to Schwab's as "headquarters." Typical of many drugstores in that period, the store had a counter serving ice cream dishes and light meals. Hollywood legend holds that Lana Turner was discovered at Schwab's fountain, although the event actually occurred at a malt shop about a mile away.

4 ounces chocolate syrup (page 17), divided
2 scoops coffee ice cream (page 10)
Whipped cream (page 20)
1 maraschino cherry

DIRECTIONS

Into a tulip sundae glass put 1 ounce chocolate syrup. Add the coffee ice cream. Cover with remaining chocolate syrup. Top with whipped cream and garnish with cherry.

Harold Arlen wrote "Over the Rainbow" while sitting in his car in front of Schwab's Drugstore.

During Prohibition, a healthy splash of hard liquor found its way into soda water glasses at some fountains, and the expression "Don't Care" became the term for these special mixtures when a customer was thirsting for a stimulant.

Chicago Sundae

3 tablespoons crushed
   pineapple, divided
2 scoops vanilla ice cream
   (page 6)
Whipped cream (page 20)
1 maraschino cherry

In 1935, Gus Poulos began serving homemade ice cream at a two-table stand called Homer's in Chicago's North Shore suburb of Wilmette. His ice cream was richer than any other in that era, anywhere in Chicago. From its humble beginnings, Homer's has grown to become the quintessential ice cream parlor, with brick walls, festive red-and-white interior, and old-fashioned ball lights. Legend has it that, after serving his term in Alcatraz in 1939, Al Capone bought a lakefront house not far from Homer's. The head of the "Chicago Outfit" visited often for an ice cream treat.

DIRECTIONS

Into a tulip sundae glass, put 1 tablespoon crushed pineapple. Add the vanilla ice cream. Cover with remaining pineapple. Top with whipped cream and garnish with cherry.

According to *White's Vest Pocket Sundae Formulary*, a similar fountain formula was called the Sunshine Sundae.

During the 1920s, servers at Chicago fountains drew a connection between the pineapple topping and the slang term "pineapple" for grenade used by Chicago gangsters, because of the similar shape and the crisscross pattern common to both.

Muddle Sundae

James Papageorge arrived in the United States as a nine-year-old stowaway from Tripoli, Greece, in 1904. He landed in Chicago, where, with hard work and determination, he earned a living by scooping ice cream at a soda fountain and selling fruit at a fruit stand. By 1920, he had saved enough money to buy Gayety's, an ice cream parlor and candy store nestled next to the Gayety Theater on Chicago's South Side. The vaudeville and feature picture showplace is long gone, but the Papageorge family continues the Gayety's tradition in suburban Lansing, where they serve the Muddle Sundae.

DIRECTIONS

Into a tulip sundae glass, put 1 ounce hot fudge. Add the vanilla ice cream. Cover with caramel. Top with whipped cream. Sprinkle with pecans and garnish with cherry. Fill a small pitcher with remaining hot fudge and serve on the side.

> Hot fudge should be kept at a temperature high enough to ensure its being in an easy-to-pour state, yet not hot enough to cause it to "sugar" after standing a few hours.

> Ingrid Bergman, already an established movie star in Europe, came to New York in 1939 when she was twenty-four. She loved hot fudge sundaes so much that she alarmed her American hosts.

4 ounces hot fudge (page 12), divided
2 scoops vanilla ice cream (page 6)
3 ounces caramel syrup (page 18)
Whipped cream (page 20)
Salted pecans, butter-roasted
1 maraschino cherry

Chop Suey Sundae

1 tablespoon raisins

1 tablespoon dates

1 tablespoon figs

4 ounces maple syrup

2 scoops vanilla ice cream
  (page 6)

Shredded coconut

1 maraschino cherry

Beginning in the mid-nineteenth century, Chinese immigrants settled their own Chinatowns within major United States cities, where they opened chowchow lunchrooms. At first these small, cramped eateries catered to their own people, then expanded their menus to attract curious Americans who dared cross into those mysterious cities-within-cities. Native cooking got mixed up with American traditions, producing this fountain concoction listed in *The National Soda Fountain Guide* (1913).

DIRECTIONS

Chop raisins, dates, and figs, and mix together with the maple syrup. Add scoops of ice cream side by side in an oval dish. Ladle the chop suey mix between the scoops and sprinkle shredded coconut over the top. Garnish with cherry.

Chop suey, a Chinese American dish prepared from "leftovers," was first offered in the 1920s as an ice cream sundae (for twenty cents) at the Chocolate Garden, a dessert parlor in Venice, California.

Soda fountain waitstaff and kitchen workers communicated orders in colorful, quirky "calls." If you were in one of these places between 1925 and 1945, you might have overheard a sundae called a "bellyache."

Waldorf Sundae

A traditional Waldorf salad consists of apples, walnuts, celery, and a mayonnaise-based dressing. The salad was created by Oscar Tschirky, the maître d' at New York's Waldorf Astoria Hotel, for the preopening of the hotel on March 13, 1893. By the 1930s, the Cole Porter musical *Anything Goes* featured a song ("You're the Top") that makes a reference to it with the line: "You're the top, you're a Waldorf salad." The popularity of the restaurant salad did not go unnoticed at the soda fountain, and was eventually reinvented as a sundae.

DIRECTIONS

Add scoops of ice cream side by side in an oval dish. In the center between the two, place a mixture of the apple and walnuts. Top with whipped cream and garnish with cherries.

> The formula for a "Waldorf Parfait" alternated layers of vanilla ice cream with crushed pineapple, crushed raspberries, chopped nuts, whipped cream, and cherry.

> Making things look nice at a clean fountain where the dispenser has good materials to work with is a matter of dexterity. Of course, they must have thin, dainty glasses, etc., because you know that a drink looks better and tastes better when served in a thin glass than when served in a thick one.

2 scoops vanilla ice cream
 (page 6)
1 tablespoon peeled and
 coarsely chopped apple
1 tablespoon chopped walnuts
Whipped cream (page 20)
2 maraschino cherries

Vanilla Poached Eggs on Toast

Sponge cake, sliced
1 scoop vanilla ice cream,
   softened
½ peach or apricot, pitted

Back in the 1940s, a soda jerk by the name of Jean Gude invented the "Fried Egg Sundae," served ever since at the fountain of Stoner Drug in Hamburg, Iowa. In its center is a scoop of cream-colored vanilla ice cream covered with marshmallow sauce, which could be construed to resemble the yolk of an easy-over egg, and it is ringed with chocolate syrup to suggest the browned edges of the white. "Vanilla Poached Eggs on Toast" was another mimic of the breakfast menu offered during the heyday of the soda fountain.

DIRECTIONS

Cut sponge cake to resemble slices of toast and spread a thin layer of the vanilla ice cream on top to resemble the white of an egg. Place half a peach or an apricot on top, round-side up, to resemble the yolk.

From *The Pacific Drug Review* (1920): "The finest concoction loses its charm if indifferently served."

According to Paul Dickson in *The Great American Ice Cream Book* (1972), "Lagging Depression-era sales prompted the industry to unveil a variety of bizarre 'sales-stimulating' ice cream combinations and do-it-yourself suggestions like this one."

Black Night Sundae

The Sealtest brand was originally a franchise, with local dairies purchasing rights to the trademark in their market areas. In the 1950s, Sealtest brand milk and ice cream products sponsored national network broadcasting, including the *Sealtest Big Top* on CBS-TV. The circus-themed show featured Ed McMahon (later famous for *The Tonight Show*) as the clown, actor Jack Sterling as the ringmaster, and Dan Luri as the Sealtest bodybuilder. National magazine ads for Sealtest promoted "The Best Ice Cream in a Month of Sundaes," including this all-chocolate sundae for the thirtieth day.

4 ounces chocolate syrup (page 17), divided
2 scoops chocolate ice cream (page 8)
Walnuts, chopped

DIRECTIONS

Into a tulip sundae glass, put 1 ounce chocolate syrup. Add the chocolate ice cream. Cover with remaining chocolate syrup and sprinkle walnuts over the top.

According to *White's Vest Pocket Sundae Formulary*, similar fountain formulas might have been called Chocolate Noodle or Chocolate Dope.

"Drop a bucket of mud with a black bottom!" That's how a waiter barked an order to a soda jerk for a double chocolate sundae. Depending on the fountain, the dish might also have been called a Black-Out Sundae or a Black Diamond Sundae.

Black & White Sundae

4 vanilla wafers

1 scoop vanilla ice cream

1 scoop chocolate ice cream (page 8)

3 ounces marshmallow sauce (page 15)

Pecans, chopped

3 ounces chocolate syrup (page 17)

Walnuts, chopped

The yin and yang of chocolate and vanilla was never more graciously displayed than in a version of the black and white sundae devised by French chef Louis De Gouy, an apprentice of the great Escoffier, and head chef at the Waldorf Astoria hotel for thirty years. In his book, *Soda Fountain Luncheonette Drinks and Recipes* (1940), De Gouy explains that sundaes should be served "daintily," and he warns: "Don't fill the sundaes too much, so full that the dressing used runs over the edge."

DIRECTIONS

Place vanilla wafers on a flat dish so as to form two squares. Dip vanilla ice cream onto one square, chocolate ice cream onto the other. Cover vanilla ice cream with marshmallow and top with pecans. Cover the chocolate ice cream with chocolate syrup and top with walnuts.

Outside of the venerable Waldorf, the classic sundae is sometimes called a Spotted Dog.

When a plain sundae is topped with a ladle of whipped cream and decorated with a cherry it is called a "French Sundae." It was customary for fountains to charge an extra five cents for these sundaes; the amount of whipped cream was generous and not to be confused with the little dab sometimes used for decoration only.

Barney Google

A long-running American comic strip created in 1919 by Billy DeBeck, *Barney Google* inspired the popular 1923 song, "Barney Google (With the Goo-Goo-Googly Eyes)," and by 1925 a banana-based ice cream sundae called "Barney Google" appeared in *The Soda Fountain Dispenser's Formulary.*

DIRECTIONS

Add 1 scoop each of vanilla ice cream and chocolate ice cream side by side onto an oval dish. In the center between the two, add the crushed pineapple. Slice the banana half into disks and place around the ice creams. Top with whipped cream and garnish with cherry.

1 scoop vanilla ice cream
1 scoop chocolate ice cream (page 8)
4 ounces crushed pineapple
½ banana
Whipped cream (page 20)
1 maraschino cherry

From *The American Druggist and Pharmaceutical Record* (1916): "The pharmacist usually experiences little difficulty in devising new sundaes and names, the chief difficulty being connected with the improvement of the older popular formulas."

Maple Walnut Sundae

3 tablespoons wet walnuts
(page 21), divided
2 scoops vanilla ice cream
(page 6)
Whipped cream (page 20)
½ walnut

In April of 1947, Carl Sponseller opened a frozen custard store in a former gas station on Route 1 in Fredericksburg, Virginia, the busiest north-south travel route in the eastern United States at the time. Although the country's interstate system has bypassed Carl's, people still wait in long lines for ice cream churned out by vintage Electro-Freeze machines. Ordering is reminiscent of the *Seinfeld* "Soup Nazi" episode. Customer-enforced protocol calls for one to approach the counter with money in hand, order decisively, and step aside quickly. Carl's Maple Walnut Sundae is a local favorite.

DIRECTIONS

Into a tulip sundae glass, put 1 tablespoon wet walnuts. Add the vanilla ice cream. Cover with remaining wet walnuts. Top with whipped cream and garnish with walnut half.

From *The Retail Druggist* (1920): "A small dish heaping full may look as though you gave more for the money than the same amount would in a larger dish."

Thanksgiving Day Sundae

The Dispenser's Soda Water Guide, published in 1909, encourages soda fountain managers to develop original recipes for "palate-tickling concoctions." Special sundaes, it explains, are similar to sheet music: "they make a hit, no one knows why, and are profitable until the fad or craving for them is worn off." The creamy white pignoli nut lends its sweet, rich flavor to the passing fancy of this holiday-inspired sundae.

DIRECTIONS

Add 1 scoop of vanilla ice cream and 1 scoop of chocolate ice cream side by side on an oval dish. Cover with chocolate syrup. Sprinkle pignoli nuts over the vanilla ice cream, walnuts over the chocolate. Garnish with cherries.

From *Let's Sell Ice Cream* (1947): "The chocolate sundae is the most asked for sundae at the soda fountain. There are enough variations to suit all tastes."

1 scoop vanilla ice cream
1 scoop chocolate ice cream (page 8)
4 ounces chocolate syrup (page 17)
Pignoli nuts
Walnuts, chopped
2 maraschino cherries

Snowball

1 scoop vanilla ice cream
   (page 6)
½ cup moist shredded coconut
4 ounces hot fudge (page 12)

In 1920s Baltimore, "Snowball" was the name for a cup of shaved ice with syrup, pieces of fruit, and marshmallow. During the Great Depression, the Snowball sold for a penny and was known as "the hard-times sundae." In better years, Snowball was the name bestowed on a favorite restaurant dessert with vanilla ice cream rolled in coconut and topped with hot fudge. No lesser an institution than New York City's legendary Stork Club featured a sundae-style Snowball on its menu in the 1940s.

DIRECTIONS

Shape vanilla ice cream into a ball and place into the freezer for about 5 to 10 minutes. Pour the coconut onto a plate. Remove ice cream from the freezer and roll in the coconut. Return to a serving dish. Cover with hot fudge.

From its inception in the Roaring Twenties as a speakeasy to its heyday in the fifties, everyone from Marilyn Monroe to J. Edgar Hoover gathered at the Stork Club.

In the 1946 film classic *It's a Wonderful Life*, Mary Hatch declared her undying love for young George Bailey at the soda fountain of Gower's drugstore. She whispered her sentiments in George's deaf ear while he prepared her a sundae with coconut sprinkles from the Fiji Islands.

Joe Sent Me

There are few things in this world that go together as well as chocolate and strawberries, as confirmed by the Joe Sent Me sundae at the Sweet Dreams Café in Stroudsburg, Pennsylvania, a historic town in the Pocono foothills. The Sweet Dreams fountain inherited the formula (and the name) from legendary Jahn's, the defunct chain of New York City ice cream parlors that coined sundae names like Boilermaker, Awful Awful, Suicide Frappe, and Screwball's Delight.

3 ounces hot fudge (page 12), divided
2 scoops vanilla ice cream (page 6)
2 tablespoons crushed strawberries
Whipped cream (page 20)
1 maraschino cherry

DIRECTIONS

Into a tulip sundae glass, put 1 ounce hot fudge. Add the vanilla ice cream. Cover with remaining hot fudge, then crushed strawberries. Top with whipped cream and garnish with cherry.

> The chief requisites necessary to the serving of a good sundae are pure, high-grade syrups, crushed fruits, and a good grade of ice cream.

> Instead of using strawberry syrup from a pump, obtain a strawberry pulp syrup, permitting the crushed or ground pulp of the fruit to remain in the syrup, and serve it from pitchers.

I.C.U. Sundae

3 tablespoons crushed
  strawberries, divided
2 scoops vanilla ice cream
  (page 6)
Almonds, chopped
Whipped cream (page 20)
Cinnamon powder

In 1914, the *Spatula Soda Water Guide* attempted to define a sundae for the drugstore trade: "A sundae is a dish of ice cream over which is poured a given syrup or crushed fruit, with or without nuts or whipped cream. The sundae is so elaborated that it becomes almost anything with ice cream in it as long as it is not a drink." In fountains of the era, the name I.C.U. (short for "I see you") lent a special aura of quality to a fancified strawberry sundae.

DIRECTIONS

Into a tulip sundae glass, put 1 tablespoon crushed strawberries. Add the vanilla ice cream. Cover with remaining strawberries. Sprinkle almonds on top and add whipped cream. Dust with cinnamon.

While the term "sundae" is universally known, the sundae possesses many local names applied to entirely different fountain preparations. In some parts of the South it was called a "lollypop."

While it is customary to decorate each sundae and dish of ice cream with a cherry, a strawberry may be used instead, selecting sound, fully ripe, dark red berries of medium size. The service is dainty and sundaes thus decorated look attractive and the public likes the change.

Brownie Bottom Sundae

History has it that the brownie was invented in Chicago by the chef of the Palmer House Hotel during the 1893 Columbian Exposition. Socialite Bertha Palmer, it seems, requested a dessert for ladies attending the fair that would be smaller than a piece of cake, and easily eaten from boxed lunches. Offered is the original Palmer House recipe for rich, "gooey" brownies, later popularized as the base for a sundae by Hot Shoppe restaurants, established in Washington, D.C., in 1927 by J. Willard Marriott, best known for founding the Marriott Corporation.

1 brownie (page 2), cut into
    4" x 4" square
1 scoop vanilla ice cream
4 ounces hot fudge (page 12)
Whipped cream (page 20)
1 maraschino cherry

DIRECTIONS

Place brownie on a flat dish. Add the vanilla ice cream. Cover with hot fudge. Top with whipped cream and garnish with cherry.

From *Drug Topics* (1920): "The soda fountain is the most valuable, most useful, most profitable, and altogether most beneficial business building feature assimilated by the drugstore in a generation."

At legendary Ghirardelli's in San Francisco, a chocolate chip cookie served under a layer of vanilla ice cream and hot fudge is called the Cookie Bottom Sundae; at Ella's Deli in Madison, Wisconsin, a slice of pound cake becomes the base of the Grilled Pound Cake Sundae.

1 scoop strawberry ice cream
(page 9)
4 ounces chocolate syrup
(page 17)
1 banana
Whipped cream (page 20)
Roasted peanuts, crushed

A story is told that a screenwriter once asked Charlie Chaplin "How can I make a fat lady, walking down Fifth Avenue, slip on a banana peel and get a laugh? Do I show first the banana peel, then the fat lady approaching, then she slips? Or do I show the fat lady first, then the banana peel, and *then* she slips?"

"Neither," said Chaplin. "You show the fat lady approaching; then you show the banana peel; then you show the fat lady and the banana peel together; then she steps *over* the banana peel and disappears down a manhole." At 1920s fountains, a backward-named version of a banana sundae was sure to follow.

DIRECTIONS

Add strawberry ice cream onto the center of a flat dish. Cover with chocolate syrup. Split the banana in half widthwise, and place each half upright on either side of the ice cream. Top each upright banana with whipped cream and sprinkle crushed peanuts over all.

From *The Bulletin of Pharmacy* (1917): "The pharmacist, with increasingly less time devoted to compounding drugs, supplemented his income by adding various elements to the drugstore. One of the most important and romanticized was the soda fountain, where the pharmacist dispensed ice cream sodas and sundaes."

Black & Tan Sundae

Ice cream parlors in America owe at least some of their popularity to Prohibition. If you couldn't indulge in booze, you could at least eat ice cream. Thus, the black and tan sundae may be a suggested alternative to the Irish black and tan, a half-and-half drink of mixed stout and ale. The 1917 *Bulletin of Pharmacy* provided a formula for the black and tan sundae, along with profitable advice to the pharmacist: "Every fountain patron is a potential buyer for other merchandise."

DIRECTIONS

Dip 1 scoop of coffee ice cream and 1 scoop of chocolate ice cream side by side on an oval dish. Cover the coffee ice cream with chocolate syrup, and cover the chocolate ice cream with coffee syrup. Top with whipped cream and garnish with cherry.

1 scoop coffee ice cream (page 10)

1 scoop chocolate ice cream (page 8)

3 ounces chocolate syrup (page 17)

3 ounces coffee syrup (page 19)

Whipped cream (page 20)

1 maraschino cherry

According to *White's Vest Pocket Sundae Formulary*, a similar fountain formula was called the Broadway Sundae.

From *The Meyer Druggist* (1921): "The dispenser need not confine himself to one specialty article; in fact, it is better to have two or three—each one with some individual advantage to attract certain tastes. And in dispensing these specialties, it is important that the quality be fully maintained."

Uncle Sam Sundae

2 scoops vanilla ice cream
   (page 6)
3 ounces crushed strawberries
3 ounces crushed pineapple
1 banana, sliced into wheels
Whipped cream (page 20)
Red, white & blue jimmies
   (sprinkles)
2 maraschino cherries

One of St. Louis's oldest and most popular attractions, Crown Candy Kitchen, was opened in 1913 by Harry Karandzieff and Pete Jugaloff, who brought their confectionary skills from Greece. During the early 1950s, Harry's son George took over, determined to maintain sundae categories long since vanished from most American fountains: A sundae is ice cream and syrup; a "Newport" includes whipped cream and nuts; a "Deluxe" adds more flavors of ice cream and/or syrups.

DIRECTIONS

Dip 2 scoops of vanilla ice cream side by side in an oval dish. Cover 1 scoop with the crushed strawberries, the other scoop with the crushed pineapple. Surround the ice cream with banana slices. Top with whipped cream, sprinkle with jimmies, and garnish with cherries.

In Missouri, the ice cream sundae is pronounced "sun-duh." According to the locals, "Sunday" is the day you go to church, and a "sunduh" is what you eat *after* you go to church.

Scotch Lassie

Joe Beerntsen worked as a candymaker in Green Bay, Chicago, and Milwaukee before opening his own confectionery in Manitowoc, Wisconsin. Still going strong, the charming candy shop and soda fountain, with a striped awning out front and handsome dark woodwork inside, is a refreshing step back into time. Slide into one of the original black walnut booths and dig into an expertly made, two-sauce sundae called the Scotch Lassie.

DIRECTIONS

Into a tulip sundae glass, put 1 ounce hot butterscotch. Add the vanilla ice cream. Cover one side with remaining butterscotch, the other with the marshmallow. Top with whipped cream and sprinkle with chopped pecans.

> According to sundae lore, nineteenth-century Manitowoc soda fountain operator George Giffy established the prescient policy of limiting sales of a yet-to-be-named ice cream concoction to a single day of the week (Sunday).

3 ounces hot butterscotch (page 13), divided
2 scoops vanilla ice cream
2 ounces marshmallow sauce (page 15)
Whipped cream (page 20)
Pecans, chopped

Dunce Cap Sundae

2 tablespoons crushed strawberries, divided

2 tablespoons crushed pineapple, divided

2 scoops vanilla ice cream (page 6)

Roasted peanuts, crushed

1 ice cream cone

Whipped cream (page 20)

The reference to a "dunce cap" first appeared in the 1840 novel *The Old Curiosity Shop* by Charles Dickens. The conical cap was used as a method of punishment through public humiliation in school classrooms. Students who were slow, lazy, or considered to be stupid were forced to sit in the corner of the classroom with a dunce cap. It was inevitable that an aspiring sundae maker would notice the resemblance between the edible cone for serving ice cream and the amusing headgear.

DIRECTIONS

Into a tulip sundae glass, put ½ tablespoon crushed strawberries and ½ tablespoon crushed pineapple. Add the vanilla ice cream. Cover with remaining strawberries and pineapple. Sprinkle peanuts over the top. Fill the ice cream cone with whipped cream, invert, and place on top.

> The ice cream cone was invented in St. Louis, Missouri, in 1904 at the Louisiana Purchase Exposition, a crisp pastry cooked in a hot waffle-patterned press coming to the aid of a neighboring ice cream vendor who had run out of dishes.

> Syrian immigrant Abe Doumar developed a four-iron machine that rolled his native *zalabia* into cones. In 1905 he opened ice cream stands at Coney Island and "Little Coney Island" in North Bergen, New Jersey, before settling in Norfolk, Virginia, where Doumar's has become something of a local legend.

Rocky Road Sundae

While 1929 may be remembered in American history as the year of the Stock Market Crash and the beginning of the Great Depression, ice cream enthusiasts may recall it as the year someone put sundae toppings *inside* of ice cream. Rocky road ice cream was created by William Dreyer, founder of Dreyer's Ice Cream in Oakland, California. The ice cream's three components, chocolate ice cream, tiny marshmallows, and toasted almonds offered a variation of an original sundae of the times.

4 ounces marshmallow sauce (page 15), divided
2 scoops chocolate ice cream (page 8)
1 teaspoon macarons, broken
1 teaspoon pecans, chopped
1 teaspoon walnuts, chopped
1 maraschino cherry

DIRECTIONS

Into a tulip sundae glass, put 1 ounce marshmallow sauce. Add the chocolate ice cream. Cover with remaining marshmallow sauce. Sprinkle macarons, pecans, and walnuts over the top and garnish with cherry.

Some say this ice cream flavor was originally invented at Fenton's Creamery (also in Oakland), with chopped candy bars including chocolate, walnuts, and marshmallows among the ingredients.

Dreyer's claims its founder named the Depression-era ice cream "Rocky Road" as an allusion to the economic rough road ahead.

Buffalo Sundae

4 ounces chocolate syrup
(page 17), divided
2 scoops vanilla ice cream
(page 6)
Whipped cream (page 20)
Walnuts, chopped
1 maraschino cherry

Claude D. Smith came to Grand Junction, Colorado, in 1900, at age twenty-one. Already a certified pharmacist, young Smith and a partner bought the Adams Drug Store on the southwest corner of 5th and Main. Smith was able to buy out his partner in less than three years, with success eventually allowing him to purchase six more drugstores located in Fruita, Grand Junction, Palisade, Debeque, and Grand Valley (modern-day Parachute). Smith's soda fountains served all the regular fountain drinks, including phosphates, and ice cream treats included the specialty "Walnut and Buffalo Sundae, both rich and smooth."

DIRECTIONS

Into a tulip sundae glass, put 1 ounce chocolate syrup. Add the vanilla ice cream. Cover with remaining chocolate syrup. Top with whipped cream, sprinkle with walnuts, and garnish with cherry.

Thomas and Charles Stoddart opened Stoddart Brothers Drug Store at 84 East Seneca Street in Buffalo, New York, the first location in the city to install a soda fountain.

Northwestern Druggist magazine (1913) described another version of the Buffalo Sundae as "chocolate ice cream, marshmallow slices, and cherries."

C.M.P. Sundae

Marshmallow became a popular sundae topping during World War II because most chocolate was being used for the armed forces, and while whole eggs were rationed, powdered egg whites were not. After the war, fountain customers were delighted to have their chocolate syrup back, but since they had developed a taste for marshmallow, a combination of both sauces began to appear. Originating in the coal region towns of Pennsylvania, the C.M.P. Sundae, adding a crunch of peanuts, became the popular favorite in local ice cream parlors.

2 scoops vanilla ice cream (page 6)

3 ounces chocolate syrup (page 17)

3 ounces marshmallow sauce (page 15)

⅓ cup roasted, salted peanuts

DIRECTIONS

Dip 2 scoops of vanilla ice cream side by side on an oval dish. Cover 1 scoop of ice cream with the chocolate syrup, and cover the other with the marshmallow. Layer the top with peanuts.

From *The Pacific Drug Review* (1920): "Serve a paper napkin (7 by 14 inches), folded once over, with all sundaes, placing the napkin under the dish or glass."

From *American Druggist Magazine* (1906): "The introduction of the sundae is credited to the soda fountain trade as it goes over the counter and it seems to be very much in favor on the part of the seller."

Mud Pie

1 slice chocolate cake
1 scoop vanilla ice cream
  (page 6)
4 ounces hot fudge (page 12)
Whipped cream (page 20)
1 maraschino cherry

Remember the coffee shop in *Pulp Fiction*? Scenes that opened and closed the film were shot on location at Pann's, the futuristic "googie-style" architectural wonder on LaTijera Boulevard in Los Angeles. Since 1958, the Panagopoulos family has served breakfast, lunch, and dinner with desserts that include a West Coast version of the Mississippi Mud Pie, a sundae resting on a slice of chocolate cake. The dessert was created in the 1950s with a dense cake said to resemble the banks of the Mississippi River.

DIRECTIONS

Place slice of cake on a flat dish. Add the vanilla ice cream. Cover with hot fudge. Top with whipped cream and garnish with cherry.

Chocolate cake crumbs become "blacktop" in the Pot Hole Sundae, a creation of Gifford's in Skohegan, Maine.

Howard Johnson's *Fountain Service Manual* offers directions on scooping ice cream: "Hold the scoop firmly, with your thumb under the release. The closer your hand is to the head of the scoop, the better leverage you have."

High School Special

Pop Tate's Chocklit Shoppe is a fictional soda shop created by Bob Montana as a setting for the characters in his *Archie* comic strip. Tate's soda fountain was based on real-life locations frequented by teenagers in Haverhill, Massachusetts, during the 1930s. The character of Pop Tate was inspired by the Greek immigrant owner of these Haverhill soda shops. In the years 1936 to 1939, when Montana went to high school in Haverhill, he would join his friends at the counter and make sketches on napkins.

2 scoops vanilla ice cream
   (page 6)
3 ounces chopped cherries
   in syrup
3 ounces marshmallow sauce
   (page 15)
Whipped cream (page 20)
Spanish peanuts

DIRECTIONS

Dip scoops of vanilla ice cream side by side in an oval dish. Cover 1 scoop with the chopped cherries, and cover the other with marshmallow. Top with whipped cream and layer with peanuts.

From *The Retail Druggist* (1920): "When you advertise a special, let it be one of such quality that you can safely guarantee it to give satisfaction."

From *The Pacific Drug Review* (1918): "Choose some drink or sundae that you want to make a run on; let two or three of the most popular high school girls and boys who come into your store try it; ask their opinions, and if they like it you can be pretty nearly certain they're going to tell the rest of the crowd about it, and before you know it, you will have calls for it regularly."

Coffee "Roon"

2 scoops coffee ice cream
2 tablespoons macaroon
   crumbs
Whipped cream (page 20)
1 pineapple cube

In 1936, Professor Harold W. Bentley of Columbia University documented the peculiarly American phenomenon of "camouflaged soda fountain language" in *Linguistic Concoctions of the Soda Jerkers*. A sign of the times, the soda jerker's effectiveness was judged in part on the basis of his ability to show off the fountain by the witty use of such lingo as "coff" for coffee ice cream, the principal ingredient in a popular "dry" sundae.

DIRECTIONS

Into a tulip sundae glass add the coffee ice cream. Cover with the macaroon crumbs. Top with whipped cream and garnish with pineapple cube.

This sundae can be made using maple or chocolate ice cream. Change name according to the flavor of ice cream used.

From *The Meyer Druggist* (1921): "The soda fountain clerk who has the ability to attract people to his fountain because they prefer to come to him for service rather than to go to some other place where they would receive just as much in quantity, has scored a victory that is worth much in the business world."

Coney Island Sundae

No other sundae name was represented by as many different formulas. The 1909 *Dispenser Soda Water Guide* described a Coney Island Sundae as: "ice cream with red cherry syrup, and whipped cream topped with orange syrup and a maraschino cherry." A year later, *The Bulletin of Pharmacy* version was: "orange sherbet in the shape of a cigar and some vanilla ice cream in the same shape; lay them together in a saucer, then top with a ladle of chopped pineapple, a ladle of whipped cream, and a cherry." Philadelphia's Franklin Fountain offers a contemporary interpretation.

4 ounces marshmallow sauce (page 15), divided
2 scoops chocolate ice cream (page 8)
1 tablespoon orange marmalade
Whipped cream (page 20)
Candied orange peel

DIRECTIONS

Into a tulip sundae glass, put 1 ounce marshmallow sauce. Add the chocolate ice cream. Cover with remaining marshmallow sauce. Spoon orange marmalade onto the top, and add whipped cream. Garnish with candied orange peel.

Proprietors Eric and Ryan Berley named their "ice cream saloon" after Philadelphia's own Benjamin Franklin, who had operated his first business nearby.

From *American Druggist and Pharmaceutical Record* (1906): "Granting a neat fountain, the druggist should have a responsible attendant. An inexperienced and slovenly attendant is always a source of dissatisfaction to customers and a detriment to the increase of the store's general business."

Co-Ed Sundae

2 scoops vanilla ice cream
2 ounces chocolate syrup
   (page 17)
2 ounces marshmallow sauce
   (page 15)
1 banana
Whipped cream (page 20)
Walnuts, chopped
1 maraschino cherry

Doumar's of Norfolk is marked by a sign with two big ice cream cones on either side, a reminder that Abe Doumar, the founder, invented the ice cream cone. You can still get your ice cream served in a freshly made waffle cone, but the co-ed sundae (called "Pride of the House") has long enjoyed canonical status at Doumar's.

DIRECTIONS

Dip scoops of vanilla and chocolate ice creams side by side on a banana split dish. Cover one scoop of ice cream with chocolate syrup, the other scoop with marshmallow. Split the banana lengthwise and place halves on either side of the ice cream. Top with whipped cream, sprinkle with chopped walnuts, and garnish with cherry.

"There are several ways of making banana splits," according to the trade publication, *What Every Ice Cream Dealer Should Know* (1914), "and many of the dealers use several of the most convenient fruits which they have on hand."

Teens of the 1920s invented dating. It was a more flexible way of meeting and seeing each other that was not as supervised as it had been in the past. Previously, boys had to be courting a girl, they had to be committed, and girls had to be engaged to them in order to go out with them.

Bone Dry Sundae

According to *The New Castle News*, a Pennsylvania newspaper, in 1916: "The sundae consists of ice cream smothered in everything except young onions. Owing to the Prohibition wave, thousands of skillful bartenders have been thrown out of employment, but most of them have since been hired to manufacture the ice cream sundae in long wriggling relays. Every few days some former barkeeper will bring out a new sundae which is harder to cook than a welsh rarebit in a hay cooker." Without a sauce or syrup, the bone dry sundae was a deviation from conventional wisdom.

DIRECTIONS

Dip scoops of vanilla and chocolate ice creams side by side on an oval dish. In the center between the two, add the shredded coconut. Top with whipped cream, sprinkle with chopped walnuts, and garnish with cherry.

> When a flat plate or platter is used, level off the ice cream scoop portion so that it will sit firmly on the dish.

> Interest in coconuts produced hardly a nod until 1895, when Franklin Baker, a Philadelphia flour miller, received a shipload of coconuts in payment of a debt from a Cuban businessman. After unsuccessful attempts to sell the cargo before they spoiled, he made a decision that put coconuts into the hands of commercial confectioners and soda fountains: he set up a factory for shredding and drying the coconut meat.

1 scoop vanilla ice cream (page 6)
1 scoop chocolate ice cream (page 8)
2 tablespoons shredded coconut
Whipped cream (page 20)
Walnuts, chopped
1 maraschino cherry

Banana Split

1 scoop vanilla ice cream
(page 6)
1 scoop chocolate ice cream
(page 8)
1 scoop strawberry ice cream
(page 9)
2 tablespoons crushed
pineapple
3 ounces chocolate syrup
(page 17)
2 tablespoons crushed
strawberries
1 banana
Whipped cream (page 20)
Walnuts, chopped
3 maraschino cherries

In 1904, David Strickler became the first to liberate the sundae from the straitjacket on a single scoop of ice cream with one topping. As a twenty-three-year-old clerk at the Tassell Pharmacy in downtown Latrobe, Pennsylvania, he framed three small sundaes with a tropical banana. The banana split's popularity was assured when Charles Walgreen made it the feature dish at the fountains of his drugstore chain.

DIRECTIONS

Into a banana split dish, add scoops of vanilla, chocolate, and strawberry ice creams. Cover vanilla ice cream with the crushed pineapple, chocolate ice cream with the chocolate syrup, and strawberry ice cream with the crushed strawberries. With the peel on, split the banana in half lengthwise. Remove peel and place halves one on each side of the ice creams, with inside cut facing out. Top with whipped cream, sprinkle with chopped nuts, and garnish with cherries.

In hash-house Greek, the abbreviated speech of soda fountain employees, the banana split was either a "houseboat" or a "farmer's lunch."

In 1907, a restaurant owner from Wilmington, Ohio, thought he made the first banana split. Unaware of the earlier invention in Latrobe, Ernest Hazard also concocted an ice cream dessert which featured a split banana. Hazard's effort is celebrated annually in Wilmington with a Banana Split Festival.

Popcorn Sundae

A 1916 issue of *The Bulletin of Pharmacy* offered a "palate tickler" called the chocolate popcorn sundae, using "well-popped corn from which all the hard unpopped kernels have been removed." The magazine assured soda fountain operators that "You will find few sundaes that will look, taste, or sell better than this one."

DIRECTIONS

Dip the chocolate ice cream onto an oval dish. Cover with 3 ounces of hot fudge. Sprinkle popped corn very liberally and cover with remaining hot fudge. Top with whipped cream and garnish with cherry.

2 scoops chocolate ice cream (page 8)
6 ounces hot fudge (page 12), divided
Popcorn
Whipped cream (page 20)
1 maraschino cherry

> During the Depression, popcorn, at 10 cents a bag, was one of the few luxuries poorer families could afford; so while other businesses failed, the popcorn business thrived.

> "The use of ice cream at the soda fountain in various sections of the country has increased enormously," according to *Confectioners Journal (1916)*. "It has become so that it is no unusual thing in certain localities for a confectioner or even a druggist to run regularly six or eight kinds of ice cream."

Merry-Go-Round Sundae

1 large scoop vanilla ice cream
   (page 6)
4 ounces chocolate syrup
   (page 17)
Animal crackers
Small paper parasol

In 1919, Hans Petersen founded an ice cream institution in Oak Park, the Chicago suburb with the highest concentration of houses or buildings anywhere designed and built by Frank Lloyd Wright, the dean of American architecture. Petersen's still retains a vintage character, serving a playful sundae inspired by the amusement park rides in old Chicago.

DIRECTIONS

On a round, flat dish, dip the scoop of vanilla ice cream onto the center. Cover with the chocolate syrup. Arrange animal crackers around the ice cream. Place the paper parasol at the top.

From a 1917 issue of *The Bulletin of Pharmacy*: "Some soda jerkers are born to be artistic, others have to learn to be. There is a knack, natural or acquired, in decorating those things that require decoration so that they look tempting."

At Petersen's, waiters jot down "chocolate O" on their order pads for a chocolate soda, and "chocolate U'" for a sundae. (Can you crack the code?)

Cracker Jill

Immortalized in the classic song, "Take Me Out to the Ball Game," Cracker Jack has earned a place in the hearts and stomachs of Americans since it was introduced at the World's Fair in Chicago in 1893. The name came along three years later when, according to legend, a salesman, upon tasting the treat for the first time, proclaimed "That's a Cracker Jack!" The name was patented and a brand was born. When Cracker Jack was added to a chocolate sundae, it was named for the other half of the nursery rhyme twosome.

4 ounces chocolate syrup (page 17), divided

3 tablespoons Cracker Jack

2 scoops vanilla ice cream

Whipped cream (page 20)

1 maraschino cherry

DIRECTIONS

Into a tulip sundae glass, put 1 ounce chocolate syrup. Add 1 tablespoon Cracker Jack, then the vanilla ice cream. Cover with remaining chocolate syrup, then add remaining Cracker Jack. Top with whipped cream and garnish with cherry.

> Cracker Jack was not the only "spoon novelty" used at the fountain. Rice Krispies were added to marshmallow topping in a Krispy Marshmallow Sundae.

> In 1910, coupons were included in Cracker Jack boxes which could be redeemed for prizes. It wasn't until 1912 that children's prizes (miniature books, magnifying glasses, tiny pitchers, beans, metal trains, etc.) were place in the boxes. The company slogan was "a prize-in-every-package."

Strawanna

3 tablespoons crushed
   strawberries, divided
1 scoop strawberry ice cream
   (page 9)
1 scoop vanilla ice cream
½ banana, sliced into wheels
Whipped cream (page 20)
1 whole fresh strawberry

A trip to Rumpelmayer's, that fabled pink ice cream parlor in the St. Moritz Hotel, was a New York holiday ritual for young girls, dressed delectably, with their festive coats and scarves and hats. The well-bred institution was famous for its marble soda fountain, pink décor, stuffed teddy bears, and sundaes of undiluted quality: the best ice cream, real whipped cream, superior fruit toppings, and French fan-shaped biscuits. Rumpelmayer's Strawanna sundae, made with fresh, ripe strawberries, was proper and restrained.

DIRECTIONS

Into a tulip sundae glass, put 1 tablespoon crushed strawberries. Add 1 scoop strawberry and 1 scoop vanilla ice cream. Place banana wheels around the top and remaining crushed strawberries in the center. Top with whipped cream and garnish with whole strawberry.

From *The New York Times* (2003): "Rumpelmayer's enjoyed a long run at the center of New York's hot chocolate universe, but it closed several years ago—more a victim of age and exhaustion than of a nation's changing tastes."

New York's legendary soda jerk, Mr. Jennings, served behind the fountain of an ice cream parlor called Hicks for twenty-six years, creating fruit-laced hot fudge extravaganzas. He once said: "First God created heaven and earth. Then he created soda fountains."

Soap Box Derby Sundae

Originally, soapbox cars were built from wooden soap (or orange) crates and roller-skate wheels, unpowered, relying completely upon gravity to move. In 1933, *Dayton Daily News* newspaper photographer Myron Scott covered a race of boy-built cars in his home community and was so taken with the idea that he acquired rights to the event. In 1934, Scott managed to persuade fifty cities across the United States to hold soapbox car races and send a champion each to Dayton for a major race, the birth of the national-scale Soap Box Derby and the inspiration for this ice cream sundae.

2 scoops chocolate ice cream (page 8)
4 ounces marshmallow sauce (page 15)
4 Oreo cookies

DIRECTIONS

Dip scoops of chocolate ice cream side by side in an oval dish. Cover with marshmallow. On the sides of the ice cream scoops place the four cookies (to represent wheels).

From *The Spatula* (1915): "Marshmallow can be used to advantage for topping fancy drinks, hot chocolate, etc.; and will be found very useful to everyone who sells ice cream or dispenses soda water."

From *American Druggist and Pharmaceutical Record* (1906): "The drugstore window is one of the best mediums for advertising the soda fountain, and in window advertising, as a general rule, one is limited to window cards. Make them as attractive as possible."

Double Feature Sundae

1 scoop vanilla ice cream
(page 6)
1 scoop chocolate ice cream
(page 8)
3 ounces chocolate syrup
(page 17)
3 ounces marshmallow sauce
(page 15)
Whipped cream (page 20)
Walnuts, chopped
1 maraschino cherry

Such a familiar icon in popular culture, the soda fountain appeared in plays and movies: people drank strawberry sodas at the fountain in *Our Town*, it appears as the place of courtship in the 1919 movie *True Heart Susie*, and Mickey Rooney and Judy Garland flirted over sodas in the 1938 film *Love Finds Andy Hardy*.

DIRECTIONS

Dip scoop of vanilla ice cream and scoop of chocolate ice cream side by side in an oval dish. Cover the vanilla ice cream with chocolate syrup, cover the chocolate ice cream with marshmallow. Top with whipped cream, sprinkle with walnuts, and garnish with cherry.

In the classic W. C. Fields comedy, *Never Give a Sucker an Even Break*, a scene that was supposed to take place in a saloon was changed to a soda fountain by the Motion Picture Production Code.

In *Flying Down to Rio*, Fred Astaire plays Fred Ayers and Ginger Rogers plays Honey Hale: "Suppose we do a number with musical swords, and we can end up cutting Honey in half?" asks Fred.

"I'd much rather split a banana split three ways," replies Honey.

Birthdae

Confections to mark the anniversary of the day of a person's birth date back as far as the Middle Ages, especially in England, where celebrants received symbolic items such as gold coins, rings, and thimbles concealed inside their cakes. Each item was associated with a prediction. For example, a person finding a gold coin in a birthday cake would supposedly become wealthy; a person discovering a thimble would never marry.

4 ounces maple syrup, divided

2 scoops chocolate ice cream (page 8)

Whipped cream (page 20)

1 maraschino cherry

2 pretzel sticks

DIRECTIONS

Into a tulip sundae glass, put 1 ounce of maple syrup. Add the chocolate ice cream. Cover with remaining maple syrup. Top with whipped cream, garnish with cherry, and put a pretzel stick into either side of the sundae.

From *The Meyer Druggist* (1921): "Always remember to handle the garnish with prongs or a spoon. Never use your fingers."

Boy Scout

2 scoops chocolate ice cream
  (page 8)
3 ounces hot butterscotch
  (page 13)
3 ounces marshmallow sauce
  (page 15)
Whipped cream (page 20)
Peppermint candy

Since their inception in 1910, the Boy Scouts of America have prepared many famous men for adulthood and even public service. The organization has followed Robert Baden-Powell's dream of transforming the youth of the world, providing them with adult companionship, tests of skill and endurance, and middle-class Protestant values emphasizing hard work, thrift, honesty, reliability, and leadership.

DIRECTIONS

Dip scoops of chocolate ice cream side by side in an oval dish. Cover one scoop with butterscotch, cover the other with marshmallow. Top with whipped cream and garnish with a piece of peppermint candy.

From *The Bulletin of Pharmacy* (1917): The true science of dispensing lies in always having your dishes come out the same.

From *American Druggist and Pharmaceutical Record* (1906): "Push a special sundae, one of your own naming, so your competitor will not steal your thunder, and push it hard, as your leader, by suggesting it when your customers ask, 'What have you?' and by advertising in your newspaper and by neat signs placed prominently on fountain and counter."

Acknowledgments

This entire work is really an acknowledgment because it is meant to express my love for Ithaca, New York, the place where I have spent my entire adult life, the place where I have made my truest friendships. *The Ice Cream Sundae Book* could not have been written anywhere else. At the heart of this book are, of course, recipes that have provided a foundation for soda fountain culture, each one dreamed up by inventive fountaineers and soda jerks. For their dedication to the ice cream arts, we will be forever grateful. Thanks to photographer Bonnie Matthews for bringing these recipes to life, and to Skyhorse editor Nicole Mele for her support and guidance. Finally, I want to acknowledge the most important people in the life of this book: the readers. Thank you!

METRIC AND IMPERIAL CONVERSIONS

(These conversions are rounded for convenience)

Ingredient	Cups/ Tablespoons/ Teaspoons	Ounces	Grams/Milliliters
Butter	1 cup/ 16 tablespoons/ 2 sticks	8 ounces	230 grams
Cheese, shredded	1 cup	4 ounces	110 grams
Cream cheese	1 tablespoon	0.5 ounce	14.5 grams
Cornstarch	1 tablespoon	0.3 ounce	8 grams
Flour, all-purpose	1 cup/1 tablespoon	4.5 ounces/0.3 ounce	125 grams/8 grams
Flour, whole wheat	1 cup	4 ounces	120 grams
Fruit, dried	1 cup	4 ounces	120 grams
Fruits or veggies, chopped	1 cup	5 to 7 ounces	145 to 200 grams
Fruits or veggies, pureed	1 cup	8.5 ounces	245 grams
Honey, maple syrup, or corn syrup	1 tablespoon	0.75 ounce	20 grams
Liquids: cream, milk, water, or juice	1 cup	8 fluid ounces	240 milliliters
Oats	1 cup	5.5 ounces	150 grams
Salt	1 teaspoon	0.2 ounce	6 grams
Spices: cinnamon, cloves, ginger, or nutmeg (ground)	1 teaspoon	0.2 ounce	5 milliliters
Sugar, brown, firmly packed	1 cup	7 ounces	200 grams
Sugar, white	1 cup/1 tablespoon	7 ounces/0.5 ounce	200 grams/12.5 grams
Vanilla extract	1 teaspoon	0.2 ounce	4 grams

Index